Bianca C. Ross

Herbert Peabody

and the magic seeds

Illustrated by Tabitha Emma Bray

Published in Australia by Halsbury Co
First published in Australia in 2020
© Text copyright 2020, Bianca C. Ross
© Design and Illustration copyright Halsbury Co
Herbert Peabody ® is a registered trademark of Halsbury Co
Printed in Australia by Ingram Spark

Contact details: hello@herbertpeabody.com

Website: www.herbertpeabody.com

Cover design, typesetting: Tabitha Emma Bray

The right of Bianca C. Ross to be identified as the Author of the Work has been asserted
in accordance with the Copyright, Designs and Patents Act 1988.
This book is a work of fiction.
Any similarities to that of people living or dead are purely coincidental.
All rights reserved. No part of this publication may be reproduced, stored in a retrieval system,
or transmitted, in any form or by any means without the prior written permission of the
publisher, nor be otherwise circulated in any form of binding or cover other than that in which
it is published and without a similar condition being imposed on the subsequent purchaser.
Ross, Bianca C.
Herbert Peabody
ISBN: 978-0-6487847-4-6
pp 24

This book is for those who believe in magic!

This is Herbert Peabody.

He is a farmer.

Today, Herbie is planting tomatoes.

First, he takes a small pot and fills it with crumbly soil.

Next, he takes the tomato seeds.

Can you count the seeds?

Herbie puts the seeds into pots and sprinkles more crumbly soil over them.

The seeds are thirsty so he gives them a little drink of water from his watering can.

Herbie puts the pots in a sunny spot and remembers to give the seeds a little drink of water every day.

The seeds begin to sprout into seedlings!

How many seedlings can you count?

Herbie takes the seedlings and plants them in his big vegetable patch.

And soon...

The seedlings grow into plants with juicy, red tomatoes.

Can you help Herbie pick the tomatoes?

Because...

The tomatoes are ready for us to eat!

Yum, yum!

The End

BOOKS IN THE HERBERT PEABODY SERIES

Picture Books

Herbert Peabody and The Funky Fruit Book

Herbert Peabody and The Edgy Veggie Book

Herbert Peabody and The Friendly Friends Book

Herbert Peabody and How Food Finds Your Fork

Herbert Peabody and The Magic Seeds

Chapter Books with Pictures

Herbert Peabody and His Extraordinary Vegetable Patch

Herbert Peabody and The Incredible Beehive

E-cookbooks

Herbert Peabody Kids Cookbook Easter Food

Herbert Peabody Kids Cookbook Christmas Food

Herbert Peabody Kids Cookbook Food to Share

And head to www.herbertpeabody.com for your FREE downloads and activities.

Bianca C. Ross

Tabitha Emma Bray

Bianca C. Ross is the biographer for Herbert Peabody, the farmer helping children grow in a happy and healthy world. With a global career in research, marketing and advertising, Bianca understands Herbie's need to help people reconnect with their food and community, and show children how this can be done in a fun way.

Herbie lives on Mulberry Tree Farm in Huffelton. Bianca lives in Melbourne, Australia.

Tabitha Emma Bray's career in graphic design and illustration spans over a decade. Her passion for making and creating began when she was a young girl, and now her stunning designs and illustrations feature in the Herbert Peabody children's book series, as well as other commercial design projects.

Tabitha lives in Orange, Australia, with her husband and two young boys.

www.ingramcontent.com/pod-product-compliance
Lightning Source LLC
Chambersburg PA
CBRC090836010526
44107CB00051B/1637